# She Persisted

SONIA SOTOMAYOR

—INSPIRED BY—

# She Persisted

by Chelsea Clinton & Alexandra Boiger

# SONIA SOTOMAYOR

*Written by*
Meg Medina

*Interior illustrations by*
Gillian Flint

PHILOMEL

PHILOMEL BOOKS
An imprint of Penguin Random House LLC, New York

First published in the United States of America by Philomel,
an imprint of Penguin Random House LLC, 2021.



Visit us online at penguinrandomhouse.com.

Library of Congress Cataloging-in-Publication Data is available.

Printed in the United States of America

HC ISBN 9780593116012
PB ISBN 9780593116029

10 9 8 7 6 5 4 3 2 1

Edited by Jill Santopolo.
Design by Ellice M. Lee.
Text set in LTC Kennerley.

*For the dreamers.*
*For the hard workers.*
*For the young ones who will lead*
*into a fairer world.*

# She Persisted

She Persisted: HARRIET TUBMAN

She Persisted: CLAUDETTE COLVIN

She Persisted: SALLY RIDE

She Persisted: VIRGINIA APGAR

She Persisted: NELLIE BLY

She Persisted: SONIA SOTOMAYOR

She Persisted: FLORENCE GRIFFITH JOYNER

She Persisted: RUBY BRIDGES

She Persisted: CLARA LEMLICH

She Persisted: MARGARET CHASE SMITH

She Persisted: MARIA TALLCHIEF

She Persisted: HELEN KELLER

She Persisted: OPRAH WINFREY

DEAR READER,

As Sally Ride and Marian Wright Edelman both powerfully said, "You can't be what you can't see." When Sally Ride said that, she meant that it was hard to dream of being an astronaut, like she was, or a doctor or an athlete or anything at all if you didn't see someone like you who already had lived that dream. She especially was talking about seeing women in jobs that historically were held by men.

I wrote the first *She Persisted* and the books that came after it because I wanted young girls—and children of all genders—to see women who worked hard to live their dreams. And I wanted all of us to see examples of persistence in the face of different challenges to help inspire us in our own lives.

I'm so thrilled now to partner with a sisterhood of writers to bring longer, more in-depth versions of these stories of women's persistence and achievement to readers. I hope you enjoy these chapter books as much as I do and find them inspiring and empowering.

And remember: If anyone ever tells you no, if anyone ever says your voice isn't important or your dreams are too big, remember these women. They persisted and so should you.

Warmly,

*Chelsea Clinton*

# SONIA SOTOMAYOR

# TABLE OF CONTENTS

CHAPTER I

# *La candela*

From the very start, Sonia Sotomayor was la candela. Just like a flame, she was warm and burned brightly, but sometimes she was hard to handle. She learned to walk when she was only seven months old. She liked to play knights with her cousins, carrying them into battle on her back. They used mops and brooms to joust. And she had a well-known habit of spying on grown-ups and listening to their conversations whenever she could.

"She is like an ají," her family said. That is the Spanish word for a hot pepper that can sometimes burn your tongue. Who would have guessed that a girl like Sonia would become the first Latina Supreme Court Justice for the United States?

Sonia grew up in the Bronx, New York. Her parents had settled there when they arrived from Puerto Rico in 1944. Sonia's mother, Celina, was a hospital nurse who worked the night shift. Her father, Juan, worked in a radiator factory. He took care of Sonia and her younger brother, Junior, after school. Other people in her family were nearby, too. Abuelita, Sonia's favorite grandmother, lived a few blocks away, just like Sonia's tías, tíos and primos. That meant there were always aunts, uncles and cousins to play with. Every Saturday night, Abuelita threw a party for the whole family in her apartment. They ate chicken and arroz con gandules. They danced and shared old poems. Sonia loved those parties, especially since she could always sleep over at Abuelita's house afterward. In the morning, she had Abuelita—and a big plate of pancakes—to herself!

But one Sunday at church, when Sonia was eight years old, she found that she was not feeling like an ají at all. In fact, she felt more like a wilted lettuce. She began to sweat. Her arms went limp. When she opened her mouth to sing, she fainted in the pew instead.

Ay! Mami and Papi were so worried. What was wrong with their little girl? They went to see their good friend Dr. Fisher right away. He asked Sonia many questions. Was she very thirsty during the day? Was she having trouble staying dry in the bed at night?

*How embarrassing*, Sonia thought. She didn't like these private questions at all. And what was he doing with that rubber hose around her arm, or that long, sharp needle?

A blood test!

When Dr. Fisher tried to prick her, Sonia ran out the door of the clinic. Nurses were chasing behind her! Sonia hid under a parked car until someone finally grabbed her ankles and dragged her back inside.

There were many days of testing in the hospital after that, but finally Dr. Fisher knew what had made Sonia faint.

"You have diabetes," he told her in his office. There was too much sugar in her blood. An organ

in her body called the pancreas was not doing its job, and this was very dangerous. Sonia was going to have to change what she ate and drank. He was sure that her bedwetting and fainting would go away once they had the sugar under control.

What Sonia didn't know at first was that she was also going to need insulin shots every day to keep her alive and healthy. Insulin would help move the sugar from her blood to other places in her body where it was needed.

Sonia's family was frightened. Abuelita thought it was a curse. And worse, Sonia's parents began having even more arguments than usual. It wasn't about how much alcohol Papi drank every day or the ugly way he behaved when he was drunk. Now the fights were about who would give Sonia her shots. Mami was a nurse, but she wasn't always home when Sonia needed insulin. Papi felt too scared of needles to give Sonia an injection by himself.

Who was going to keep Sonia healthy?

It was Sonia who came up with a solution.

She had always watched adults carefully, and now, at last, it was going to pay off.

"I will give myself the shots, Mami," she told her mother.

"Do you know how?" her mother asked, surprised.

"Yes."

Sonia turned on the stove with a match. *Whoosh!* The blue flame appeared. She boiled the needle in water to kill the germs, just like she'd seen her mother do. She measured the medicine and made sure there were no bubbles inside the syringe. Then she gave herself her insulin shot so that no one would have to argue again.

C H A P T E R 2

## *Creciendo y aprendiendo*

Sonia hated school at first, but who could blame her? For one thing, she wasn't a very good student. Plus, she had to force herself to stay quiet and still—especially if she didn't want to get in trouble with her teachers at Blessed Sacrament.

Her teachers were nuns who wore bonnets and black robes called habits. They were very strict about behavior—*too strict*, in Sonia's opinion. They punished students harshly for breaking even little rules. They didn't listen to explanations when someone got blamed for something they didn't do. An angry flame inside her burned whenever that happened. *It's not fair*, Sonia thought as she stared in silence out the window. Rules and punishments should always be fair.

Still, Mami and Papi insisted that good discipline was important. A private Catholic school like Blessed Sacrament was just what they wanted. They worked hard to save money to pay for her schooling every year.

It was Papi's job to get Sonia and her brother, Junior, ready for school every day. One morning, when Sonia was in the third grade, Papi sent them on their way as usual, but he was not feeling well at all. He felt so sick that he decided to stay home from work.

That afternoon, during recess in the schoolyard, Sonia stopped playing and looked toward the apartment building where her family lived. Even though she didn't know it then, terrible trouble was happening there. When she and Junior walked home later that day, the rest of her family was gathered together and crying. They told her that Papi had gotten very ill and was taken to the

hospital. All the heavy drinking he had done over the years had hurt his body. He had died at the hospital that afternoon.

Sonia's whole world changed after that day. It was as if the bright light inside her got snuffed out. A terrible loneliness fell over the whole family. The parties at Abuelita's house stopped. Her mother dressed herself in black and stayed in her bedroom with the door shut. She barely spoke to Sonia and Junior for days . . . and weeks . . . and then months.

Sonia was so lonely that she started to fill her days with reading. She had never liked books before, but now she found that she could escape into the pages of a story. Soon, the Parkchester Library became her favorite place to forget her sadness.

Still, not even books could stop her from

wondering if there would ever be happy times again. What would happen to her and Junior if Mami stayed sad forever? Who would help them grow up?

Finally, Sonia couldn't stand it anymore. Her mind was burning with so many worries. She went to her mother's bedroom door and banged on it. "You've got to stop this!" she shouted. "You're miserable and you're making us miserable, too!"

Those fiery words were just what Mami needed. In the days and weeks that followed, she opened the shades on the windows to let in light and turned the radio back on. She changed into cheerier clothes. She moved them to a new apartment, and started improving her English, too. She even bought Sonia a set of encyclopedias so that she and Junior could read about anything they

were curious about—everything from new ideas in space exploration to the most unusual animals in Africa. It was time to learn to live without Sonia's father.

The next few years at Blessed Sacrament were much better. Sonia still missed Papi, of course, but school didn't seem so bad anymore. All that time spent reading books by herself had fanned a tiny new flame inside her. Now that she was a stronger reader, learning felt easier. She even wanted to earn gold stars from her teachers like some of her classmates. The trouble was, she didn't know how to be a good student.

Sonia gave her problem some thought. A person could learn things from books, but maybe they could also learn from all sorts of people, not just from teachers. She decided to ask Donna, the best student in her class, to teach her how to take notes and how to study for tests. It worked! Soon, Sonia's chart was crowded with glittering stars. She had become one of the best students in her class, too.

# CHAPTER 3

## *Sueños*

Sonia had never really thought of what jobs she might like as an adult. That was because doctors didn't think she'd grow up at all. Back then, they believed that people with diabetes didn't live very long.

But those ideas were changing as Sonia was starting middle school. Treatments were getting much better, and now doctors knew that people with diabetes could live very long and happy lives if they took good care of themselves.

Sonia was determined to do just that.

She started to dream about her future with the help of books and TV. Her favorite book series was Nancy Drew. The stories were about a young girl detective who solves crimes with the help of her two best friends. Sonia liked how Nancy Drew had to figure out mysteries like puzzles.

Sonia also liked a popular TV show called *Perry Mason*. The show was about a lawyer who defended people who were wrongly accused of a crime. What Sonia liked most about the *Perry Mason* show was the judge. The judge sat behind a tall desk and kept order with a little hammer called a gavel. The judge listened very carefully to both sides of a case and decided if a person was guilty or innocent. The judge had to be fair when choosing the right punishment for the crime. It could not be too harsh, and it could not be too easy.

Sonia thought she might like to be a detective like Nancy Drew or a lawyer or judge like the ones on *Perry Mason*. She knew she was smart enough. After all, her friends now called her "Compy," which was short for "computer-head," because she did so well in school.

But there was still one big obstacle. Sonia was terrified of speaking in front of people. She had learned to be quiet at Blessed Sacrament because she didn't want to get in trouble. Now the idea of speaking up like Perry Mason scared her.

Sonia thought hard about her new problem and decided that she needed practice. She volunteered to do Bible readings in church. Back then,

not many girls read in church. Mostly, the service was handled by priests, with altar boys as helpers. But Sonia signed up anyway. Her hands shook with fear and her knees knocked together as she walked to the pulpit the first time. Her voice sounded wobbly in that big church where everyone's eyes were on her. But when Sonia finished the reading, her eyes were burning bright. She knew she could do it again.

By the time she started ninth grade at Cardinal Spellman High School, she signed up for all sorts of activities she thought would build her confidence. She became a maritime cadet with students who wanted to be in the armed forces one day. Sonia didn't want to be in the navy, but she still liked marching in uniform as part of the Puerto Rican Day Parade. She ran for student council and invited her friends over to her apartment to make signs for their campaigns. And most important, she joined the forensics team with her friend Kenny Moy.

The forensics team helped students learn how to debate. Debate is a special way of arguing about an idea using facts and logic to prove your point. The coach assigns a debate topic, such as whether students should have homework every night. There are two sides. One that is arguing for the idea—yes, students should have homework—and one that is arguing against the idea—no way, students should not have homework. The team that presents their point of view the best is the winner.

Sonia became an excellent debater. She liked reading and doing research to learn as much as she could about the debate topic. She enjoyed piecing together the puzzle of her own ideas so that

everything made sense. She liked listening carefully to what the other team was arguing so that she could defend her point of view better. Even how she used her hands to talk—a habit that Kenny thought she should change—became part of how Sonia won debates.

## CHAPTER 4

# *En la lucha*

By the time Sonia was a sophomore in high school, she wanted to get a part-time job. She didn't want to be bored in the summer months, with only her reading list to keep her busy. Besides, Mami had gone back to nursing school to get more education. Sonia wanted to help earn money for rent and food until Mami was working full-time as a nurse again.

Sonia's first job was at a clothing store called

United Bargains. Her salary was one dollar per hour, which was very little, but Sonia didn't mind. She liked working with her aunt Titi Carmen. She also enjoyed keeping the piles of clothes tidy, checking the dressing rooms, and helping customers.

But not all parts of the job were fun. The shop was in a neighborhood that was unsafe. After closing time, Sonia and Titi Carmen pulled the steel grates down over the shop windows and started their walk home. Police officers watched from rooftops with guns ready to stop people from stealing, lighting fires, or hurting others.

Another part of the work that Sonia didn't like was that she sometimes had to stop people from stealing clothes. She would check their bags and tell them to put back what they had stolen. Most people looked ashamed when she caught them.

Sonia tried to be fair and think of their mistake from their point of view. She knew that stealing was wrong, but she also knew they didn't have the money to pay for what they needed. Good people could lose their way and make very bad decisions.

That was even true about the police.

One day, while she was buying a banana from a man with a fruit cart, a police car pulled up to the curb. The man quickly filled a bag with his best fruits and handed it to one of the officers. Then they drove away without paying.

"Why didn't you charge him?" Sonia asked.

He explained that if he didn't give the police their fruit for free, he wouldn't be allowed to sell fruit from his cart at all.

This was wrong, Sonia thought. The police were not supposed to take gifts for special favors.

They were breaking the rules and being unfair when they were supposed to uphold the rules and treat everyone fairly.

This made her think about one of the books she was reading from her summer list. It was called *Lord of the Flies*. It was about a group of boys who find themselves shipwrecked without any adults to set up rules and laws. Soon they begin to quarrel and hurt one another until no one can get along. Sonia decided that rules were important. Everyone needed to follow rules and laws in a community. Everyone needed to think and care about fairness to others in their community.

Sonia's next job was at Zaro's Bakery, which was across the street from her family's new apartment in Co-op City. Zaro's was a kosher bakery, but it reminded Sonia of her tío's bakery in Puerto

Rico, where she used to visit as a little girl and sometimes help with customers. In this new neighborhood, Sonia met many people who were not Puerto Rican. They didn't speak español or eat tamales and beans, like her family. She learned about other foods and languages. She also noticed that even when people were from different countries, they weren't so different from each other. People loved their families. They enjoyed their neighbors. They told stories and came together to celebrate around holidays. Sonia thought that it wasn't hard to find things to like about people, if only you bothered to get to know one another.

But Sonia was also discovering that not everyone felt so welcoming about people's differences. Around that time, Sonia began dating a classmate from Cardinal Spellman named Kevin Noonan, who would become her husband years later. Kevin came from an Irish family in Yonkers, New York. His mother knew that Sonia was smart and hard-working, but she did not like that Sonia was Puerto Rican. Sonia knew this was wrong.

Disliking people because of where they come from was not a fair way to judge people. Now more than ever, Sonia believed that it was important to be fair.

CHAPTER 5

# *Tentando nuevas vías*

When it was time to pick a college to go to after high school, Sonia's old friend from forensics club, Kenny Moy, gave her important advice. He thought she should apply to the very best schools in the country. Sonia visited many good schools. Some felt too fancy. Others were very far away.

But Princeton, in New Jersey, seemed just right. Many important people, like James Madison, the fourth president of the United States, had gone to Princeton before her. She liked that it was close to home. And she thought the campus was beautiful, too, with old buildings and big trees, just the way she had always imagined a college should be.

Best of all, her friend Kenny already went to Princeton and could help her get settled. Sonia applied for admission.

After a few months, a letter arrived saying that she had been accepted. Mami was so proud! When the nurses at the hospital heard the news, they chipped in money so Sonia could buy herself new shoes for school. This was a special occasion, they said. After all, only the top students ever got accepted to Princeton.

But some people were surprised by Sonia's accomplishment. Some people were even annoyed. They thought that Princeton had offered Sonia a special favor by accepting her. They thought other students should have gotten accepted instead. They didn't think a poor Latina girl from the Bronx could do the work at such a hard school. Sonia had to hold on to the light deep inside her. She decided that she would prove those people wrong.

Her first days at Princeton, however, were not easy. She felt like she didn't belong, and soon she was homesick. The people who loved her tried to help. Abuelita sent her an envelope every week with a dollar bill inside. Sonia's boyfriend, Kevin, made trips from his college to see her on the weekends. He brought her treats to her from their old neighborhood in the Bronx. And even Mami came to visit sometimes, having a big slumber party on the dorm floor.

But it was still hard for Sonia. She noticed that many of her fellow students came from rich families. That meant that they didn't need part-time jobs to help pay for their studies the way she did. It also meant that they had gone on vacations to places Sonia had never seen. They knew about books and art and other topics that she hadn't learned about during her time growing up in the Bronx. She had learned many important things living and working in her old neighborhood, but there were also many new things she would have to learn to keep up at Princeton. She found her way to a place that had saved her before: the library. It was there that Sonia promised herself to fan her own flame. She would never stop learning about things that were new and unfamiliar to her. She would be a student of the whole world for life.

As she settled into her second year at Princeton, things seemed to get better. But then Abuelita's envelopes suddenly stopped arriving. Sonia knew something was wrong. She called

Mami and learned that Abuelita was sick in the very same hospital where Sonia had been born. Sonia rushed home that Christmas to be with her, but Abuelita died shortly after Sonia arrived.

Abuelita's death felt almost as sad as Papi's death years earlier. But Sonia remembered how Mami had locked herself away in her room. She remembered what sadness could do to a person. So, she focused on her schoolwork to help herself feel better. She joined clubs where she met students from all different parts of the world. She helped high school students from Latinx families visit the campus so they could apply to Princeton, too. She helped start a class on Puerto Rican history and helped convince the college to hire more Latinx professors and workers. She organized volunteers to be translators at a nearby hospital. She found a way to feel happy again by using her light to brighten the way for others.

By the time she was ready to graduate, Sonia had become a strong leader. She was awarded the highest honor Princeton University gives to students. It was the Moses Taylor Pyne Honor Prize. Things were looking bright for Sonia. She was heading to Yale Law School in the fall to fulfill her dream of becoming a lawyer, just like Perry Mason. And that summer, she and Kevin got married, too.

Sonia knew that Abuelita would be proud of all she had done.

# CHAPTER 6

## *Su legado*

Sonia was one of the best students at Yale Law School, but when she graduated, she did not take a job that offered her the most money or the fanciest office. Instead, she took a job working on criminal cases in New York. Sonia felt that her life in the Bronx had prepared her for understanding how and why some people came to break certain rules. She knew that it was important to treat those people fairly, even when they had done something very wrong.

Sonia's dream of becoming a judge never stopped flickering, though. To be a good judge, she would need to learn about other kinds of law, too. So, after a few years, she went to work at a law firm, where she focused on civil law. Civil cases were disputes between people or businesses over money or a person's rights.

Soon, important people in government began to notice her success. Senator Patrick Moynihan of New York was the first to recommend her to be a federal judge in 1992. As a young judge on the Southern District of New York, Sonia listened to many cases, including one that even saved major league baseball. An argument between baseball

team owners and their players had gone on so long that the World Series was canceled in 1994. Sonia ruled in favor of the players and made everyone get back to work.

Soon after that, President Bill Clinton appointed Sonia as a judge on an even higher court, the United States Court of Appeals. She was confirmed by the Senate and began that role in 1998.

But it was on May 26, 2009, that Sonia received the greatest honor for a judge in America. President Barack Obama nominated Sonia to be an associate justice of the Supreme Court.

The Supreme Court is the highest court in the United States. It is made up of nine justices who make final decisions on cases that have not been settled in lower courts. Their decisions are ideally fair and give equal justice under the law.

The justices are also experts in the Constitution, which is America's most important legal document. The Constitution describes what powers the government has and what rights citizens have in the United States. Supreme Court justices are supposed to make sure that their final decisions honor exactly what the Constitution says.

Senators debated Sonia's nomination for ten weeks. They knew that a justice keeps their job for life. They wanted to know all about her before deciding yes or no. When the votes finally came in, sixty-eight senators voted yes, and only thirty-one voted no. Sonia Sotomayor would become the first Latina justice in our history and only the third woman at that time to ever serve on the Supreme Court.

Her dreams had come true!

On August 8, 2009, Sonia was sworn in as a justice. Sonia's mother held the Bible on which Sonia took her oath of office. Her brother, Junior, who was now a doctor, was with her, too. Members of her family came from New York and Puerto Rico. Everyone wanted to celebrate Sonia's amazing achievement. The girl who had once been a

flame that was too hot to handle was now a shining light for others.

Today, Justice Sonia Sotomayor continues to serve on the court. She also writes books for adults and children, and she speaks to many groups about the law. Although she is no longer married to

Kevin, she remains close with her family, especially her nieces and nephews.

Most important, she still believes in fairness and in being a student for life. "With every friend I've known, in every situation I've encountered, I have found something to learn . . . With luck, there will be plenty of time ahead for me to continue growing and learning."

## HOW YOU CAN PERSIST

*by Meg Medina*

If you are someone who might want to be a lawyer or a judge one day—or just want to gain confidence like Sonia Sotomayor did, here are some things that you can do.

1. Get together with your friends to raise money to support research on Type 1 diabetes. You can design your event here: https://www2.jdrf.org/site

/SPageServer?pagename=diy_homepage.

2. Talk to your teachers about starting a debate club in your classroom or at your school. Here are some possible topics to debate: Should homework be banned? Should kids be allowed to drink soda? Should every home have a pet?
3. Practice speaking in front of others. You can do this by auditioning for your school play, doing the morning announcements or serving as a reader at your place of worship.
4. Be a student of the world. Read as much as you can to learn about places, people and things that are not familiar to you. Knowing about many things will help you better understand complicated ideas and situations.

5. Volunteer with an adult family member or friend for an organization that helps people in your community. You can host a book drive, help at a food pantry or volunteer at an animal shelter, for example. You'll learn how to work together with others to make your community stronger.
6. Become part of the safety patrol at your school. You'll help students remember to follow rules that keep your school safe and orderly.
7. Consider running for student government or other important jobs at your school. You'll learn how to connect with others and how to make decisions that affect a whole community.

## Acknowledgments

For the strong ones with light burning inside them. And for Justice Sonia Sotomayor, who has given us all a North Star to follow.

# References

"About the Court." Supreme Court of the United States. https://www.supremecourt.gov/about/about.aspx.

"Background on Judge Sonia Sotomayor." The White House, Office of the Press Secretary, May 26, 2009.

Collins, Lauren. "Number Nine: Sonia Sotomayor's high-profile début." *The New Yorker*, January 4, 2010. https://www.newyorker.com/magazine/2010/01/11/number-nine.

Gregory, Sean. "How Sotomayor 'Saved' Baseball." Time.com, May 26, 2009. http://content.time.com/time/nation/article/0,8599,1900974,00.html.

"Our Government: The Constitution." WhiteHouse.gov. https://www.whitehouse.gov/about-the-white-house/the-constitution.

"Portrait of: Supreme Court Justice Sonia Sotomayor." NPR Latino USA, October 9, 2018. https://www.npr.org/2018/10/08/655664271

/portrait-of-supreme-court-justice-sonia
-sotomayor.

Savage, Charlie. "Sotomayor Confirmed by Senate, 68–31." *The New York Times*, August 6, 2009. https://www.nytimes.com/2009/08/07 /us/politics/07confirm.html.

"Sonia Sotomayor Fast Facts." CNN Library, updated June 16, 2019. https://www.cnn .com/2013/03/08/us/sonia-sotomayor-fast-facts /index.html.

Sotomayor, Sonia. *My Beloved World*. New York: Alfred Knopf, 2013.

Sotomayor, Sonia, and Delacre, Lulu. *Turning Pages: My Life Story*. New York: Philomel Books, 2018.

MEG MEDINA is a *New York Times* bestselling and award-winning author who writes for children and teens. She is the 2019 Newbery Medal winner for her novel *Merci Suárez Changes Gears.* When she is not writing, she works on community projects that support Latinx youth. She lives with her family in Richmond, Virginia.

Photo credit: Sonya Sones

You can visit Meg Medina online at
megmedina.com
or follow her on Twitter
@meg_medina
and on Instagram
@megmedinabooks

GILLIAN FLINT has worked as a professional illustrator since earning an animation and illustration degree in 2003. Her work has since been published in the UK, USA and Australia. In her spare time, Gillian enjoys reading, spending time with her family and puttering about in the garden on sunny days. She lives in the northwest of England.

*Courtesy of the illustrator*

You can visit Gillian Flint online at
gillianflint.com
or follow her on Twitter
@GillianFlint
and on Instagram
@gillianflint_illustration

CHELSEA CLINTON is the author of the #1 *New York Times* bestseller *She Persisted: 13 American Women Who Changed the World*; *She Persisted Around the World: 13 Women Who Changed History*; *She Persisted in Sports: American Olympians Who Changed the Game*; *Don't Let Them Disappear: 12 Endangered Species Across the Globe*; *It's Your World: Get Informed, Get Inspired & Get Going!*; *Start Now!: You Can Make a Difference*; with Hillary Clinton, *Grandma's Gardens* and *Gutsy Women*; and, with Devi Sridhar, *Governing Global Health: Who Runs the World and Why?* She is also the Vice Chair of the Clinton Foundation, where she works on many initiatives, including those that help empower the next generation of leaders. She lives in New York City with her husband, Marc, their children and their dog, Soren.

*Courtesy of the author*

You can follow Chelsea Clinton on Twitter
@ChelseaClinton
or on Facebook at
facebook.com/chelseaclinton

ALEXANDRA BOIGER has illustrated nearly twenty picture books, including the She Persisted books by Chelsea Clinton; the popular Tallulah series by Marilyn Singer; and the Max and Marla books, which she also wrote. Originally from Munich, Germany, she now lives outside of San Francisco, California, with her husband, Andrea, daughter, Vanessa, and two cats, Luiso and Winter.

Photo credit: *Vanessa Blasich*

You can visit Alexandra Boiger online at
alexandraboiger.com
on follow her on Instagram
@alexandra_boiger

Don't miss the rest of the books in the

# She Persisted series!